Alessandro Aparecido Sandrini

The evolution of cellular systems

Alessandro Aparecido Sandrini

The evolution of cellular systems

The Evolution of Cellular Systems Vol. 1

ScienciaScripts

Imprint
Any brand names and product names mentioned in this book are subject to trademark, brand or patent protection and are trademarks or registered trademarks of their respective holders. The use of brand names, product names, common names, trade names, product descriptions etc. even without a particular marking in this work is in no way to be construed to mean that such names may be regarded as unrestricted in respect of trademark and brand protection legislation and could thus be used by anyone.

Cover image: www.ingimage.com

This book is a translation from the original published under ISBN 978-613-9-66117-6.

Publisher:
Sciencia Scripts
is a trademark of
Dodo Books Indian Ocean Ltd. and OmniScriptum S.R.L publishing group

120 High Road, East Finchley, London, N2 9ED, United Kingdom
Str. Armeneasca 28/1, office 1, Chisinau MD-2012, Republic of Moldova, Europe
Printed at: see last page
ISBN: 978-620-7-98440-4

I dedicate this book to my parents, who supported me at all times and invested in my education, and to my wife Solange, who was always by my side supporting and encouraging me at all times, because without her constant encouragement, I couldn't have finished this book.

ACKNOWLEDGEMENTS

I thank God for always being present in my heart and thoughts at every moment of my life, and also all the professionals at Delta System who helped me in any way.

To my beloved children, with you I discovered what love is. The source of my life's inspiration. You made me grow as a human being, you made me want to be a better person, you made me want to make the world a better place.

SUMMARY

The range of new possibilities built into mobile phones has only become possible thanks to the enormous technological advances that the sector has undergone in recent years. From the first analogue handsets, technology has evolved to the second generation, digital systems, and today it is reaching the 4.5G level, the fourth generation of mobile phones.

In reality, the evolution of mobile telephony has unfolded in different technologies in terms of the technical quality of their operations and the possibility of services. The digital systems that first established themselves on the market are TDMA, CDMA and GSM.

And finally, the big difference lies in the availability of new functions, which mean that mobile phones are no longer just a phone but an electronic support for the most diverse actions

Keywords: Technological advances

SUMMARY

INTRODUCTION

From the first generation of mobile communication systems to the present day, we have seen the emergence of various technological standards. Some proprietary and others open, both subject to competition and market evaluation. The range of new possibilities built into mobile phones has only become possible thanks to the enormous technological advances that the sector has undergone in recent years. From the first analogue handsets, technology has evolved to the second generation, digital systems, and today it is reaching 3G level, the third generation of mobile phones.

In reality, the evolution of mobile telephony has unfolded in different technologies in terms of the technical quality of their operations and the possibility of services. The digital systems that first established themselves on the market are TDMA, CDMA and GSM.

And finally, the big difference lies in the availability of new functions, which mean that mobile phones are no longer just a phone but an electronic support for the most diverse actions

Objective

The aim of this work is to provide basic technical information on existing mobile service technologies, to discuss the combination of mobile phones and the Internet, to show how these technologies work and some wireless technologies that influence the Wap process.

Work structure

The work is divided into 5 chapters, where we first talk about the evolution of mobile communications, giving an overview of the three generations of mobile systems, then we talk about WAP technology, its history, how it works, as well as its benefits and disadvantages. It also shows the difference between WAP and the Web and, in this chapter, a comparison is also made between them.

The next chapter discusses some wireless technologies. The 4th chapter presents the current panorama of cellular systems in Brazil.

And finally the concluding chapter.

CHAPTER 1

The Evolution of Mobile Communications

1.1 First Generation Mobile Systems

Since its first generation, the mobile phone service has worked by dividing a city or region into small geographical areas called cells, each of which is served by its own set of low-power radio transmitters and receivers. When a call from a mobile phone reaches a transmission and reception tower, it is transferred to the regular fixed telephony system. Each cell has several channels in order to provide services to many users simultaneously. As a user moves around the city, their mobile phone signal automatically switches from one cell to another without interruption.

AT&T's Bell Laboratories developed the concept of the mobile phone in 1947, and in 1970 AT&T itself proposed the construction of the first high-capacity cellular telephone system, which became known by the acronym AMPS (**Advanced Mobile Phone Service**). On 13 October 1983, the first cellular system in the US went into commercial operation in Chicago. However, NTT (**Nippon Telephone & Telegraph**) had anticipated this by putting a system similar to AMPS into operation in 1979 in Tokyo, Japan.

In Europe, the first generation of cellular systems was made up of several systems: NMT (**Nordic Mobile Telecommunications**), adopted by several countries other than the Nordic ones, TACS (**Total Access Communications System**) in the UK, Italy, Austria, Spain and Ireland, C-450 in Germany and Portugal, Radiocom 2000 in France and RTMS in Italy. All these systems were very similar to each other, with the main differences centred on the use of the frequency spectrum and the spacing between channels. AMPS, for example, operates in the 869-894 MHz band for reception and 824-849 MHz for transmission; NMT-450 operates in the 463-468 MHz band for reception and 453-458 MHz for transmission while NMT-900 uses the 935-960 MHz band for reception and 890-915 MHz for transmission, etc. With regard to channel spacing, we can mention, for example, AMPS which uses 30 kHz, TACS and several others which use 25 kHz [www.3g.com.br].

This first generation of cellular systems was basically analogue, using frequency modulation for voice and FSK *(Frequency* **Shift Keying**) digital modulation for signalling. Access to the channel is obtained through FDMA (**Frequency Division Multiple Access**). The size of the cells is between 500 metres and 10 kilometres, and *"hanhnff"* or *"annOverr"* is allowed (allowing automatic transfer of calls from one cell to another). It also allows *"nnmning"* (automatic transfer of calls between systems) between different service providers, provided they adopt the same system.

1.1.2 Band A and Band B

The A and B bands are different frequency ranges of radio waves. These frequencies are signal transmission channels. Mobile phones operate via radio waves on one of these frequencies, with analogue or digital technology.

These frequency bands are defined by international and national organisations that assign each type of service a part of the spectrum (radio wave space, where various services pass through: TV and radio stations, communication between aeroplanes and airports, and radio amateurs). These parts of the spectrum are called "frequency bands". In this way, one service cannot invade another that is located in a different band. Mobile cellular telephony in Brazil uses the 800 MHz frequency band, which is divided into two bands, A and B.

1.2 Second Generation Mobile Systems

Due to the pressure of demand, particularly in the US, where the analogue system had reached the limit of its capacity in the largest metropolitan areas, and the need to have a Pan-European system in Europe, it was necessary to start developing digital systems which, in principle, in addition to greater capacity, offered the following advantages over analogue: more powerful digital voice coding techniques, greater spectral efficiency, better voice quality, easy data communication and significantly easier encryption of the information transmitted.

"As a result of this effort, the GSM *(Giom/ee Speciale Mobile/Global System for Mobile Communications)* system emerged in Europe, TDMA *(Time Division Multiple Access)*, CDMA *(Code Division Multiple Access)* in the USA and PDC *(Japanese Personal Digital Cellular)* in Japan.

TDMA works by dividing the time of a channel, which operates on a given frequency, into a number of parts and assigning each of the various telephone conversations to each of these parts.

CDMA, a strong competitor to TDMA, is a proprietary system developed by the company QUALCOMM, based in San Diego, USA. The system uses the spectral spreading technique and was originally used by the military to spread the signal over a very wide spectrum band, making transmissions difficult to intercept or even interfere with." [www.3g.com.br]

There is also *Broadband* CDMA (B-CDMA), the patents for which are held by the company InterDigital. Essentially, B-CDMA operates by sharing the frequency spectrum with other existing cellular technologies.

"GSM was adopted as a European standard in the mid-1980s and introduced commercially in 1992, operating in the frequency range 935-960 MHz for reception and 890-915 MHz for transmission. GSM has an open architecture, which allows equipment from different manufacturers to be combined, thus making it possible to keep prices low. In its favour, there is also a large infrastructure already in place worth more than 50 billion dollars, with more than 150 GSM-900, DCS-1800 and PCS-1900 cellular networks with more than 57 million subscribers in 98 countries; more than 45 million subscribers are concentrated in Western Europe alone (23 countries). GSM is today arguably the most popular standard implemented worldwide." [www.3g.com.br]

To summarise, second-generation communications services are based on high-performance systems, some with at least three times the capacity of first-generation systems. They are generally characterised by the use of digital technology for both voice and signalling transmission.

In addition to the cellular systems seen so far, there is another line of development, known as "*cordless systems*" or "*cordless telephones*". These systems have experienced varying degrees of success over time and are in use in millions of homes around the world.

"It is estimated that there are more than 60 million cordless phones in the US, of all different types and/or models. Their use was considered illegal in Europe in the 1980s, although there were certainly a considerable number of handsets operating in thousands of homes. A European standard then emerged, CT1 (Cordless Telephone 1), with 80 channels, operating in the 914-915 MHz (mobile to base) and 959-960 MHz **(base to mobile)** bands.**" [www.3g.com.br]

Several new standards followed on from CT1 and were considered digital in that they digitised voice traffic for transmission over the air interface. One of their main attractions is the quality of the signal, which is sent at a rate of 32 kbit/s - conventional digital mobile systems generally adopt rates of up to 13 kbit/s. These standards include CT2 **(Cordless Telephone 2)**, DECT **(Digital European Cordless Telephone)**, PHS **(Personal Handyphone System)** developed in Japan and PACS **(Personal Access Communications Services)** proposed by Bellcore in the USA.

The CT2 is designed for use in domestic and business environments and can be used as a teleprompter, i.e. it offers the user the possibility, when they are close to suitably equipped booths or poles, of joining the common public telephone network. DECT offers a wireless communications structure for high traffic density, short-distance telecommunications and covers a wide range of applications and environments. PACS supports voice, data and video imaging services for indoor and microcell use.

As a response to the poor quality of service offered by analogue systems, their inability to match capacity to demand and the elitism of their services due to exorbitant prices, the PCN **(Personal Communications Network)** concept emerged in England in 1989. **The** *Department of Transport and Industry (DTI),* the

The government responsible for the UK's telecoms sector launched a consultation process on the development of a radio system that would provide high-quality two-way telecoms services for fixed and mobile environments at an affordable cost. The target was the mass market, potentially consisting of millions of users, thus promoting competition with the mobile phone system. The system's architecture would be supported by a large microcellular structure to make it possible to use low-power terminals that were therefore light enough to be carried in a **pocket**. The most suitable frequency band would be between 1.7 and 2.3 GHz, as it is less congested than the conventional mobile phone band, around 900 MHz, and the additional attenuation of the new band would be compensated for by the smaller size of the cells. In the US, this service, which is increasingly intended to be a means of communication between people rather than places, has become known as PCS (**Personal Communications Service**). The term PERSONAL is seen as key in marketing terms because it captures the imagination and inspires freedom, individuality and something tailor-made. Operators see this solution as a way of improving the services they already offer, which **currently include mobile phones, *"papeóp"*** and the conventional fixed telephony network itself.

In Europe, the first PCS applications appeared at the end of 1993 with the DCS-1800 system, a GSM variant operating with lower power and in a higher frequency range. In January 1998, there were around 3.7 million subscribers to this technology in Germany, France and the UK alone.

1.2.1 Analogue vs Digital

The difference between the systems is the high quality of the connection. In the analogue system, the sound travels via radio waves and is subject to variations, as in FM radio and TV transmissions. The connection is subject to noise and interruptions. In the digital system, although the sound is also transmitted via radio waves, it is encoded using a binary numbering system, just like computer language. As the speed is very high, the fidelity of the voice signal can be maintained.

1.2.2 CDMA Digital System

Initially, the system available was analogue, and the AMPS (Advanced Mobile Phone Service) standard was adopted in the Americas. Over time, the limitations of occupying the frequency spectrum, shortcomings in terms of the confidentiality of conversations and the diversity of analogue standards adopted in various countries meant that new standards had to be sought. From the 1980s onwards, **Global System Mobile Communications** (GSM) was developed, a digital standard for mobile cellular telephony that was a great success in Europe. In the evolution from the analogue AMPS standard to the digital standard, two technologies emerged: TDMA and CDMA.

"Code Division Multiple Access (CDMA) technology is the most suitable for densely populated urban areas, as it allows up to ten simultaneous calls to be transmitted on the same radio channel, on the same frequency and in the same time interval.

The difference between CDMA and TDMA (Time Division Multiple Access) technologies is that the latter uses different time intervals between conversations, allowing up to three subscribers on the same radio channel." [www.3g.com.br]

In CDMA digital technology, sound is coded and calls receive a code that differentiates them from other calls. This guarantees privacy and security in your calls, as it reduces the risk of interference and virtually eliminates crossed lines.

1.2.2.1   Advantages of CDMA

- **Transmission quality:** excellent voice quality. The voice doesn't sound tinny, there's no echo or interruptions.

- **Better coverage, allowing greater mobility:** with dual coverage, digital and analogue, on the same device, it is possible to be served by the analogue system in places where the digital signal is not yet available.

- **Battery life:** greater performance in digital areas. One battery can be used for up to 3 hours of conversation or two days on standby (check the specifications for each model).

- **Supplementary Services:** In addition to excellent quality Voicemail, CDMA offers Call Waiting, Consultation and Conference, Temporary Call Transfer and alertcall services.

- **Security and privacy:** It's practically impossible to track and listen in on your phone calls.

1.2.3   GSM

In the 1980s, analogue mobile phone systems were developed in Europe, especially in Scandinavia, the UK, France and Germany.

Various systems were developed, which led to incompatibilities between them due to the way data was sent, protocols and communication frequency. In 1982, **the "Cow/èrewce o/ *ECEopTan PoEIP and***

Te/egrapAs" (CEPT) was **held**, where a group called ***"Grovp SGScioI MoSile"*** (GSM) was formed to study and develop a mobile system that complied with certain standards:

- Good voice quality

- Spectral efficiency

- Small terminals and low costs

- Support for **international *roaming***

- **Capacity to support "handhe/d" terminals**

- Support a wide range of new services and utilities

- IDSN compatibility

In 1989, responsibility passed to **the European Telecommunication Standards Institute** (ETSI), where the GSM specifications were published in 1990. A GSM network is made up of various entities with specific functions and interfaces. The GSM network can be divided into three parts: the mobile station, the base subsystem station and the subsystem shown in the following figure.

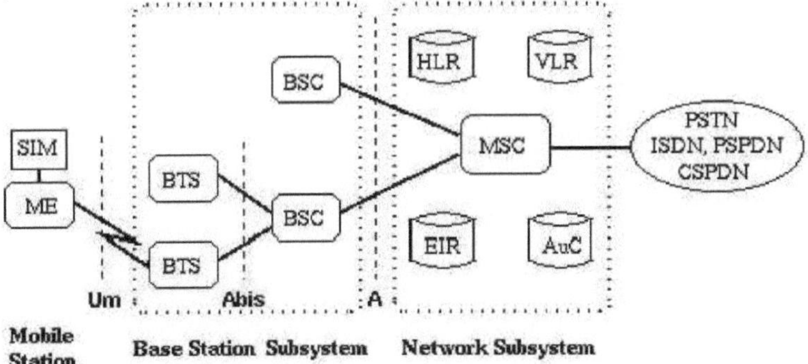

Figure 1: Structure of a GSM network

The Mobile Station Mobile equipment (terminal) and a smart card called SIM The card provides personal mobility, so that the subscriber can access the subscribed services regardless of the terminal used, i.e. by inserting the SIM card into a different terminal, the subscriber can enjoy the services from that terminal. The SIM card has a worldwide unique identification (IMSI), as does the terminal (IMEI). These codes are independent, allowing for greater mobility and personal security against unauthorised use.

The Base Radio Subsystem is responsible for controlling the radio link with the mobile station. It is divided into two parts: the transmitting base station (BTS) and the controlling base station (BSC). Communication between these two stations is carried out via the standardised Abis interface, allowing (as with the rest of the system) operation between components made by different suppliers. The BTS houses the radio receiver-transmitters that define the cell and support the radio link protocols with the mobile station. In a **large urban area, the number of BTSs is likely to be greater. The BSC manages** the resources for one or more BTSs, such as radio channel configuration, frequency hopping and *hand-offs*. *The* BSC makes the connection between the mobile stations (mobiles) and the mobile switching centre (MSC).

The main component of the Network Subsystem is the MSC, which is responsible for switching calls between mobile stations or between a mobile station and a fixed terminal. It behaves like a PSTN or ISDN switching node, and additionally provides all the necessary functionality for handling a mobile subscriber, performing registration, authentication, location updating, transition between cells (**hand-off**) and managing a **roaming** subscriber. These services are provided in conjunction with various functional entities that together form the network subsystem: MSC, HLR, VLR, EIR, AuC. The HLR, VLR and MSC together provide the **roaming** capabilities of GSM.

The HLR (**Home Location Registrer**) contains all the administrative information of every subscriber registered in the corresponding GSM network, together with the location of the mobile station. The location of the mobile station is usually in the form of the VLR (**Visitor Location Registrer**) address. The information provided by the VLR is needed to control the call and provide services to each subscriber located within a certain control area. Two other registers are used for security and authentication.

The EIR is a database containing listings of all valid mobile equipment on the network, where all mobile stations are identified by IMEI. An IMEI is considered invalid if it is declared stolen or incompatible with the network. The AuC is a protected database that stores a copy of each SIM's code, which is used to authenticate and encrypt over the radio channel.

Channel and voice coding Voice in GSM is digitally coded at a rate of 13 Kbps (260 bits every 20 ms). With the subsequent addition of error correction code, we now have a rate of 22.8 Kbps (456 bits every 20 ms). These 456 bits are divided into 8 blocks of 57 bits, resulting in 8 successive time slots being sent to protect against transmission errors. Each send is 156.25 bits long and contains 2 blocks of 57 bits and a 26-bit training sequence used for equalisation. Each send is transmitted in 0.577 ms for a total rate of 270.8 Kbps, and is modulated using GMSK on a 200 kHz carrier. Error control and equalisation contribute to the robustness of the radio signal against interference and attenuation in transmission. The digital nature of the TDMA signal allows the use of various processes to improve transmission quality, battery life and spectral efficiency.

Another feature of GSM is power control, which minimises the transmission power of the mobile stations and the BTS, thus minimising the interference generated on the channels and consumption.

The GSM system and the systems based on it, DCS1800 (operating at 1.8 GHz) and PCS1900 (operating at 1.9 GHz), are a first step towards a truly personal communication system. The SIM card brought personal mobility and mobility to the terminal. Together with international **roaming** and support for a wide variety of services such as voice, data transfer, fax, SMS and others, GSM comes close to fully satisfying personal communication needs. As such, it will be used as the basis for the UMTS project. Another noteworthy feature of GSM is its compatibility with ISDN.

1.3   Generation Systems 2.5

1.3.1   EDGE (Enhanced Data rates for Global Evolution)

This is a technology that allows GSM networks to support and offer third generation mobile telephony services. EDGE was developed to enable the transmission of large amounts of data at high speed rates (384 kbit/s). EDGE uses the same concept as TDMA (**Time Division Multiple Access**) technology, in terms of frame structure, logical channels and 200kHz bandwidth, as current GSM networks. In this way, EDGE allows current networks and 3G to coexist within the same frequency spectrum.

Offering 3G mobile internet services using your existing cellular infrastructure represents a major advantage. EDGE is the easiest way to achieve high-speed data transmission - whether on a stand-alone network or in combination with WCDMA.

EDGE has a new modulation technique which, together with improvements to the radio protocol, allows operators to use the existing frequency spectrums (800, 900, 1800 and 1900) more effectively. EDGE supports data, voice and application services at rates of up to 384kbits/s.

1.3.2   1xEV-DO

1xEV-DO was developed to operate on a 1.25MHz carrier, occupying the same amount of spectrum as previous CDMA systems (**cdmaOne, cdma2000 1x**).

Due to the similar Radio Frequency characteristics, it is quite natural to integrate 1xEV-DO with existing CDMA networks by reusing ERB infrastructure (antennas and transmission and reception equipment).

These similarities also allow manufacturers of 1xEV-DO terminals to take advantage of the significant CDMA market (174 million users), producing 1xEV-DO handsets that are already commercially available at reduced costs.

This advantage of 1xEV-DO should not be underestimated, considering that other 3G technologies will not be able to take advantage of any economies of scale during the first few years of deployment.

1.3.3 Dedicated channel for IP packages

Another advantage of 1xEV-DO is that allocating a frequency channel to carry only IP packets results in a much more efficient use of network resources, allowing data transmission of up to 2.4Mbps on the **downlink**, as well as being the first step towards an **All-IP** structure.

1.3.4 450MHz, 850MHz and 1.9GHz frequencies

The 1xEV-DO is prepared to operate in the 450MHz, 850MHz and 1.9GHz frequency bands, facilitating implementation by operators who already have a licence for these bands.

In comparison, WCDMA (the European 3G standard, also called UMTS) will initially allow downloads of a maximum of 384kbps (rel.99), and later up to 2Mbps (rel.4) using entirely a 5MHz band (where it would be possible to implement 3 1xEV-DO carriers) with the additional disadvantage of requiring new government licences in the 2.1GHz spectrum.

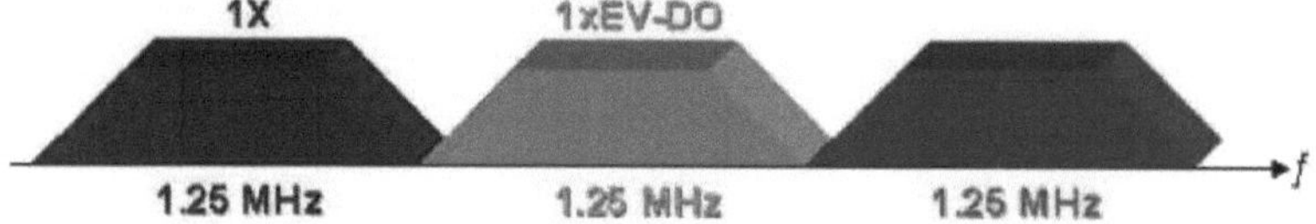

Figure 2: Carrier allocation in a cdma2000 and 1xEV-DO system

1.4 Third Generation Mobile Systems

Even though second generation systems are not yet fully mature and firmly established, intensive work is already underway to develop the third generation. This work is once again being led by Europe and sponsored by ITUR (International Telecommunications Union - Radiocommunications sector) and ETSI (European Telecommunications Standard Institute). The aim is to create a third generation mobile system, which is being called UMTS (Universal Mobile Telecommunications System).

Significant progress has already been made, such as the reservation of 230 MHz **of spectrum, with** THE **approval of 127 countries at the** World *Administrative Radio Conference* (WARC) in 1992.

"The likely topology of this new system will be based on a form of mixed cell architecture; variable-sized cells will be implemented with sizing appropriate to specific geographical areas and depending on different traffic demands. Smaller cells, i.e. picocells, installed indoors, will be improved versions of current *"oordless"* technologies, with *"anmdeets"*, i.e. subscriber handsets, that are quite small and light; larger cells, i.e. microcells and macrocells, will be able to operate according to characteristics evolved from GSM. Different *"Haddeets"* will need to recognise and operate indistinctly on pico, micro and macrocells. In other words, the aim is to create a

WIRELESS network platform, offering users the possibility of access, via radio waves, as an extension of the office telephone system when they are at work, or as a conventional mobile telephone when they are away, or even as the main telephone in their homes when they are at home." [www.3g.com.br]

The evolution towards universal mobile telecommunications services, UMTS, will most likely be based on the GSM structure. Economically and technically speaking, the creation of an independent standard for UMTS would be unjustifiable given the huge investment in making the digital cellular networks already in use viable.

"The aim of UMTS is to provide a universal standard for personal communications with mass market appeal and quality of service equivalent to the fixed network. In the UMTS vision, a communications system will have to support various facilities:

(1) relocatable carriers, bandwidth assignable on demand (e.g. 2 Mbps for indoor communications and at least 144 Kbps for outdoor environments);

(2) variety of traffic types sharing the same medium;

(3) appropriate charging for multimedia applications;

(4) personalised services;

(5) ease of implementing new services (for example, using smart grid tools);

(6) Broadband WLL (Wireless Local Loop). Narrowband WLL has been used to replace copper wires/cables to connect telephones and other communication devices to the public switched telephone network, or PSTN (Public Switched *Telephone Netwaok)."* [www.3g.com.br]

Specifically with regard to UMTS, three issues are of paramount importance:

(1) broadband radio access;

(2) intelligent *roarniiig^;*

(3) high capacity.

GSM, in its natural evolution, is fully capable of meeting these requirements as well.

"ETSI delegates meeting in Paris on 29/01/98 agreed to the adoption of a third generation air interface standard incorporating elements of two technologies: W- CDMA *(Wideband Cade Divisian Multiple Access) and* TDMA/CDMA (hybrid of Time *Divisian Multiple Access/Cade Divisian Multiple Access)."* [www.3g.com.br]

Designing a personal product such as a subscriber terminal for a mobile phone or PCS is also becoming a growing challenge for the industry. Terminals have become smaller and lighter, batteries have lasted longer and the new models that emerge always have a host of new features and functionalities.

Hewlett-Packard Co and others are trying to concentrate all the functions of a telephone onto a common credit card. British Telecom's research labs in the UK are developing a personal communicator as a garment that combines video, telephony, data communication and a personal digital assistant, known as a PDA

(*Peosanal Digital Assistant*). Sony has been working for years on a system that translates in real time, so that people from different countries can have a normal conversation in different languages. In addition, all this processing power is to be concentrated on a single chip.

"AT&T, a division of *Wioeless Services,* is introducing a device that allows users to send and receive data on a mobile network and receive e-mails on the terminal itself equipped with a *liquid* crystal display (LCD) with capacity for three lines." [www.3g.com.br]

The integration of computer technology with communications and solid-state electronics should form the basis for multimedia systems with fantastic processing powers.

CHAPTER 2

WAP Technology

2.1 WAP and its history

"The roots of WAP are quite interesting, as they were created on the premise of co-operation between industries. This is somewhat ironic, since the first version of the protocol took place at the height of the "browser wars". This co-operation was undoubtedly one of the biggest drivers behind WAP's widespread acceptance, allowing standards to be quickly developed and integrated into many existing products from many of the companies responsible for its development. This open standard also led to the emergence of many initiatives focussed on the development and *marketing of* its niche applications." [www.wapforum.org]

In 1995, when Ericsson began an effort to develop a general protocol that could offer a variety of services for wireless networks. Other companies were soon on Ericsson's heels, developing other technologies to compete with this exploding market, including two major competitors, Nokia and Phone.com, formally known as *Unwired Planet.*

The WAP protocol began its history in June 1997, when companies such as Ericsson, Nokia, Motorola *and* Phone.com joined forces in a non-profit industry association to create the WAP Forum, which was open to any company interested in participating.

These companies have created a set of protocols that define operation, security and transactions, enabling operators, manufacturers and developers to meet the requirements of flexibility and differentiation that the world of wireless telecoms is increasingly demanding.

"There are more than 100 companies from the most different sectors of the industry, such as handset manufacturers, operators, service providers, software manufacturers, content providers and companies developing services and applications for wireless devices.

It should be made clear that the WAP protocol was not developed solely to transmit content over the Internet, as any company can transmit information via other devices with no connection to the Internet. On the other hand, it is certain that the greatest growth in this technology is due to its close relationship with the world wide web." [Demétrio, 2000, p.5]

2.1.1 The Objectives of the WAP Forum

- Bringing advanced data content and services to mobile phones and other wireless terminals;

- Create a global protocol specification that will work across different wireless network technologies;

- Enable the creation of content and applications that run across a variety of networks and devices;

- Embracing and extending standards and technology where appropriate.

2.2 Definition of WAP

According to Demétrio [Demétrio, 2000, p.3] WAP stands for **Wireless Application Protocol**. It is a specification for a set of communication protocols with the aim of standardising the way wireless devices such as mobile phones, palm tops and radio transmitters/receivers access the Internet.

This protocol allows mobile access to information and services available on the Internet or private Intranets, as well as other information systems, via mobile devices. In other words, in a few days you'll be able to find out from your mobile phone which films are showing at the cinema in your town, or even find out in advance what your favourite TV channel is showing.

It's a technology that allows mobile phones to surf the Internet very efficiently. The information is compressed so that it can circulate more quickly through the network, despite the slow connection offered by these devices.

Previously, each manufacturer used a different technology. From now on, devices and services that use WAP will be able to interact. It's an open standard; it's not controlled by any one company. Any person/company can develop WAP devices and content, which ensures its use as democratic, open and universal.

Browsing WAP pages is a very similar way to the Web, using a mobile phone equipped with a **microbrowser** that reads pages created with a language called WML.

WAP technology establishes a much more solid point between the world of mobile telephony and the Internet, offering the capacity to transmit a wide range of services and content completely independent of the technology used. The great success of WAP has been to put many of the services previously confined to the use of a desktop microphone in the user's pocket, opening the door to a new world of possibilities for wireless communications (read checking your bank account balance or receiving emails, for example).

"WAP can be used on any operating system, including popular handheld platforms such as Palm OS, Windows CE and Java OS. It is also compatible with Windows 95/98/NT, Linux, Solaris. This is because the protocol is dependent on communication standards rather than being platform-based. Any platform capable of implementing communication standards is compatible with WAP." [Demétrio, 2000, p.4]

2.3   How it works

The main idea behind WAP technology is to access Internet content and services. However, only sites that have been built in WML will be correctly visualised.

"The mobile phone accesses the Internet in the same way as a computer. The handset receives an IP number (its identifier on the Internet) from the operator, and from then on, it is already part of the Internet, as it is connected to the Internet via the internal modem in the handset, in the same way that a computer is." [www.palmland.com.br]

Not all mobile phones have a **microbrowser**. Only models compatible with WAP technology can access the network.

How the WAP model works:

Table 1: How the WAP model works

0 user requests the WAP page they want to view by typing the address into their WAP mobile phone.	Dispositivo Wap
0 mobile phone *microbrowser* sends the request with the URL of the requested page and the subscriber information to the *Gateway* (software capable of connecting to the mobile phone network and the Internet).	Red de Telefonía Móvil
0 *Gateway* examines the request and sends it to the server where the requested information is located.	Wap Gateway
0 server locates the required URL and sends the information back to the *Gateway*.	Internet

At the *Gateway,* the response from the server is examined, the WML code is validated for errors and the response is generated and sent to the mobile phone.	
The *microbrowser* examines the information received and if the code is correct, displays it on the screen.	

2.4 The Benefits and Disadvantages

The benefit is a standard user interface: the interface is independent of the terminal used, similar to web pages that can be viewed on any platform, with any operating system (Mac, Windows, Unix, Linux).

- **Availability of the service:** as it is a wireless service, it allows users to request information at any time and from anywhere.

- **Wide availability of terminals:** having an open standard allows any manufacturer to incorporate its technology into their phones.

- **Multiple applications:** in recent years, the Internet model has proved to be the cheapest and most effective way of distributing information to an ever-increasing number of people. This allows WAP users to access a wide range of information.

- **To mobile phone operators:** WAP technology promises to cut costs and increase the number of subscribers simply by improving existing services and creating an unlimited number of new services and applications. Some operators already offer the service of receiving e-mails and transmitting **short messages (SMS, described below). "New services can be** implemented easily and quickly without the need for additional infrastructure or modifications to the phone. They also allow operators to differentiate themselves from their competitors by offering personalised services (some operators **provide a variety of news, such as sports and stock market quotes)."** **[Demétrio, 2000, p.7]**

- **Content providers** (newspapers, magazines) will find a rich market of potential customers for their advertisers on WAP. Consumers will be able to target products specific to their region or state.

On the downside, they have very small navigation screens with space for just a few lines. WAP mobile phones have a slightly larger screen than current ones, but it's not the same as surfing the web.

Unintuitive keyboards.

Monochrome image formats. Maybe in the future there will be colour images.

No multimedia support. Film and sound lovers will have to wait a little longer.

The main inconsistencies of this technology, i.e. the seven deadly sins:

1. **The consumer experience is poor:** Browsing WAP is like venturing back to the days of the BBS: a combination of slow access, no images and no colour. You can never get straight to the point like on the web. Access reaches a maximum of 14.4 Kbs.

2. **WAP is still insecure:** The user is the most vulnerable character in the WAP universe. If you forget or lose your device, anyone can read the bank statements and personal information stored on the phone. There are no passwords to access the **minibrowser** or e-mails.

3. **High bills:** The price of consumers' bills is inversely proportional to the size of the screen. Mobile phones themselves aren't expensive, it's the tariffs that are.

4. **Services are still irrelevant:** despite the proliferation of WAP addresses, there are still few really useful services that work without the connection failure message.

5. **Where the business model lies:** so far, only operators and manufacturers of mobile phones and **gateways** have figured out how to extract money from WAP. Due to the size of the screen, advertising is impossible. Adverts are too intrusive, the exact opposite of what happens on the web.

6. **Development is expensive:** The lack of standardisation in mobile phones, **browsers** and protocols has an economic implication: development costs will skyrocket. When developing applications, you have to work with different interfaces and optimise the content to the limitations of mobile phones. It's almost impossible to build applications that run exactly the same on different types of devices.

7. **Marked for death:** WAP, as it exists today, is a limited protocol and will have to go through a whirlwind of adaptations to cope with the third generation of mobile phones, the so-called 3G.

2.5 Difference   And Comparison Wap - Web

Viewing a WAP page is not like viewing a web page, due to the difference in screen size. But the navigation is basically the same, with a **home page** with **links** to other pages.

A WAP mobile phone cannot display web pages and a web browser cannot display WAP pages unless you use an emulator (programmes that simulate the mobile phone screen on a PC).

2.5.1 The Web Model

Web architecture provides a very flexible and powerful model. Applications and content are presented in standard data formats and navigated by applications called Web **browsers**. The web **browser** is a network application. For example, it sends requests for data objects to a network server and the server responds with data encoded using standard formats.

The Web specifications show many of the mechanisms needed to create a general-purpose environment, including standardisation of the naming model. All servers and content on the Web are named with a standard *Internet Uniform Resource Locator* - URL.

Content typing: All content on the Web has a specific format allowing *browsers* to correctly process content based on its format.

Standardisation of content formats: All *browsers* support a set of content standards - HTML, *JavaScript* and other formats.

Standardisation of protocols: Protocol standards allow a *browser* to communicate with a web server - The most widely used standard is HTTP (*HyperText Transfer Protocol*).

Figure 1 shows how a client requests a resource available on a server identified by a URL.

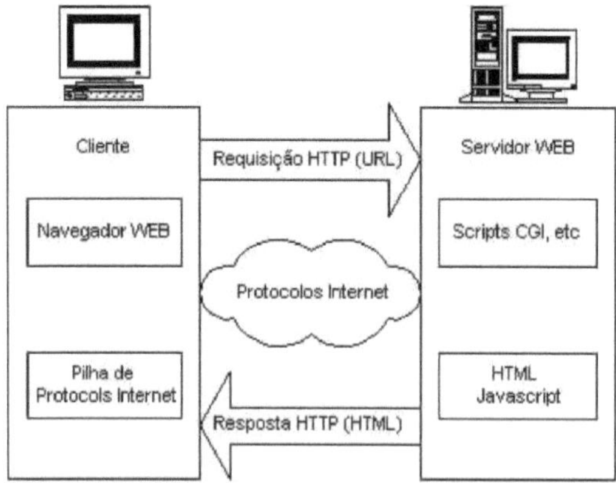

Figure 3: Service Request in the Internet Model

2.5.2 Web protocols

Web protocols define three classes of servers:

- **Origin Server:** The server where content exists (resides) or will be created.

- **Proxy:_** An intermediary programme that acts as both client and server for the purpose of executing requests acting in place of a client. A **proxy** resides between a client and a server that has no means of communicating, such as through a **firewall**. Requests are executed or passed through the **proxy**, with or without translation to other servers.

- **Gateway:** A server that acts as an intermediary for another server. Unlike a **proxy**, a **Gateway** receives requests as if it were the server from which the resource originated. The client may not be aware that it is communicating with a **gateway**.

2.5.3   The WAP Model

Services created using HTML would not be very suitable for wireless devices due to the characteristics of the environment. A markup language with characteristics very similar to HTML was then produced called WML (**Wireless Markup** *Language*), which offers a navigation model designed for devices with a small display area and limited input facilities.

To make better use of bandwidth, the WML file is encoded in a binary compressed format by a WAP **Gateway/Proxy**, which is the entity that connects the mobile domain to the Internet. In order to offer functionality comparable to that of **JavaScript, WMLScript** was created, which is a **scripting** language for WAP devices.

Figure 2 shows the WAP programming model. The basic difference to the Internet model consists of the **Gateway** that receives the client's request via the WSP protocol and converts it into an HTTP request to the destination server.

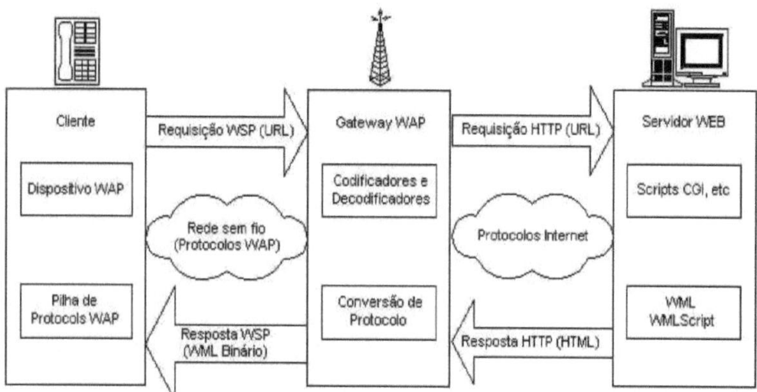

Figure 4: Service Request in the WAP Model

2.5.4 WAP - Web comparison

Providing Internet services over a **wireless** network presents new challenges for everyone involved in this activity. The market is different and consumers have new **needs and expectations.** "The *wireless* **network** has less bandwidth and some communication difficulties. The devices used are also different, mainly because they have less memory, less processing power, a smaller screen and **limited data input** capabilities." **[www.wapbrasil.cjb.net]**

The Internet is widely used today. Many people use it to find information of all kinds. Examples of services available are access to banking, shopping and exchanging information with like-minded people.

Although these services and even some applications are different, the process is the same.

A request is sent from a computer to a web server via the Internet. The server interprets the request and sends the response to the computer that requested it, where it will be displayed.

See the basic operating diagram in figure 3.

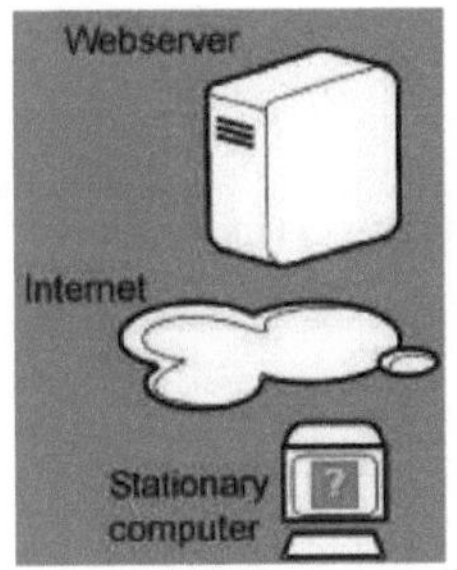

Figure 5: Web Communication Model

WAP has been developed in such a way that any compatible device can access applications and services specially developed for this environment via the Internet.

The WAP device (a mobile phone, for example) sends a request via the **wireless** network to a WAP **Gateway**. The **Gateway** converts the request into a web protocol and sends it to the web server.

The web server sends the response to the **Gateway** where it is converted and encoded, and sent over the **wireless** network to the device that originated the request, where it is displayed.

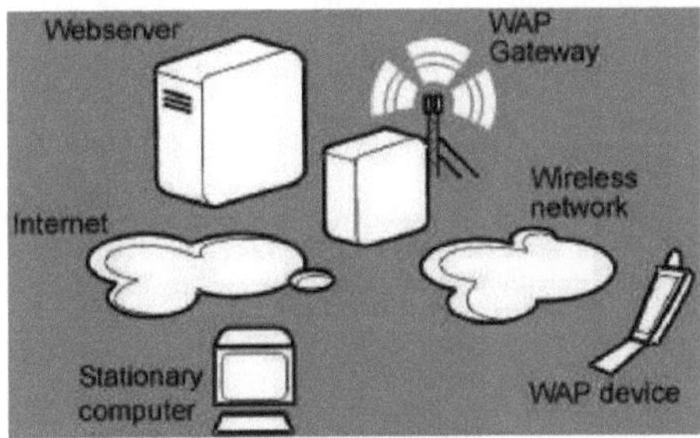

Figure 6: WAP Communication Model

The WAP specification applies to most **wireless** devices today. It also uses the best of existing Internet standards at the same time as new standards are developed.

Table 2: Comparing WAP and Web

	Web	WAP
Access mode	Computer with modem	GSM mobile phone
Screen size	800 x 600 *pixels*	4 x 3.5 cm
Handling	Mouse, keyboard	Screen touches, keyboard
Easy to use anywhere, anytime	No	Yes
Multimedia (sounds, videos)	Yes	No
Programming Language	HTML, *JavaScript*	WML, WMLScript

2.   6Wap architecture   and security

2.6.1   WAP architecture

WAP allows information and services to be sent easily to mobile users, regardless of time and place. A WAP device is required to access these services. A WAP device can be a mobile phone, a PDA or a **handheld** computer.

To visualise information and services over the **wireless** network, the WAP device needs to have a WAP **browser** installed, called a **microbrowser**.

"The *browser* interprets and displays content developed for the WAP environment. This content is created using WML (**Wireless Markup** Language). WML is similar to HTML, which is used to create websites. But unlike HTML, WML was created to meet the needs of *wireless* devices and networks." **[www.testecell.hpg.ig.com.br],**

To add dynamic features to WML applications, the *WMLScript* language is used, a language similar to *JavaScript*. Both WML and *WMLScript* are adapted and optimised for the *wireless* environment.

WML content consists of one or more *cards* and is not built like web pages. WML uses *cards* and *decks* to specify its content. A *card* is usually a unit of interaction with the user and a *deck* would be the same as a page.

The WAP standard defines an application environment and application protocols. It also defines the technology known as WTA (*Wireless* Telephony *Application*).

The purpose of WTA is to provide the means to create telephony (voice) services using WAP. The interface between the telephony-related functions on the WAP device is called WTAI (*Wireless* Telephony *Application Interface*).

When the WAP *browser* is used to request information, the URL request is sent using the WAP protocols. This request is sent via the *wireless* network to the WAP *Gateway*. The *Gateway* allows users of the *Wireless* network to connect to the Internet.

When the incoming request is decoded, the *Gateway* performs a number of tasks. Then the decoded request is converted from the WSP protocol (in the WAP standard) to the HTTP Internet protocol.

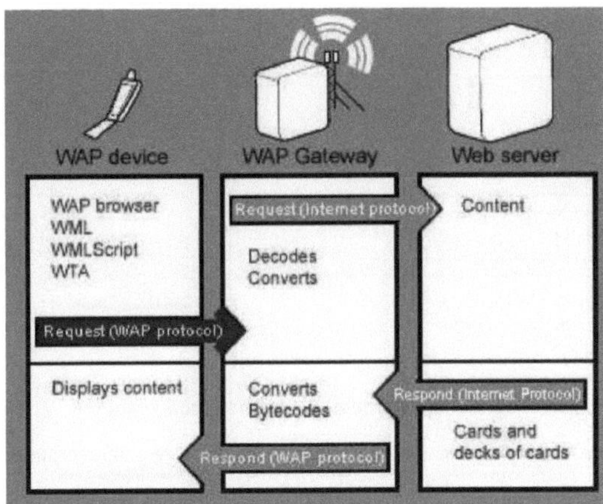

Figure 7: WAP content request and response

What happens next is that the request is sent to the Web **server** over the Internet. The Web **server** receives the request, reads it and returns a response with WML content to the WAP **Gateway**.

The WAP **Gateway** receives the WML content from the web server and converts it into the WAP **bytecode** standard, encoding the information into a binary format so that less bandwidth can be used. This reduction can vary from 40 to 70 per cent.

The encrypted content is sent over the **wireless** network to the WAP **browser**. The **browser** receives the response from the WAP **Gateway** and displays it on the WAP device's screen.

2.6.2 WAP architecture components

"The WAP architecture is made up of a scalable and extensive environment for developing applications for mobile communication devices. This is achieved by means of the WAP protocol, which is made up of several layers of sub-protocols, each layer of which can be accessed by the upper layer and by other services and applications." [Demétrio, 2000, p.8]

Below is a diagram of the layered protocols:

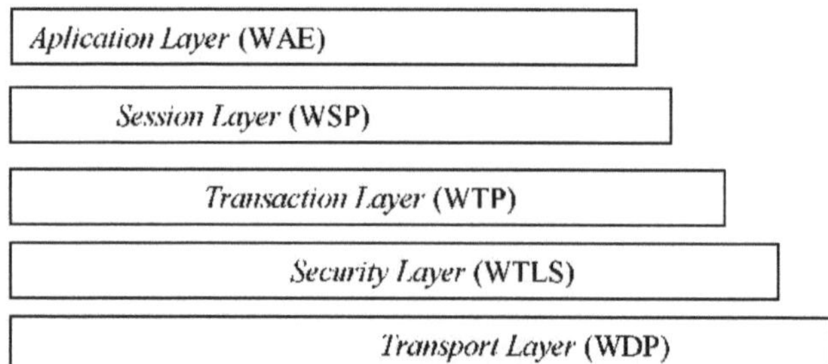

Figure 8: Layers of the WAP Protocol Stack

The WAP layer architecture allows other services and applications to use the functions of the WAP layer stack via well-defined interfaces. In addition, external applications can directly access the session, transaction, security and transport layers.

2.7 WAP Protocol Stacks

2.7.1 *Wireless Application Environment* (WAE)

A general-purpose application based on a combination of WWW and mobile telephony technologies. Its main objective is to establish an interaction between Operators and Service Providers, to allow applications to be built efficiently, regardless of the device on which they will be executed (mobile phones, palmtops).

WAE includes a **microbrowser** with the following functions:

- WML, a lightweight, optimised language similar to HTML, but specifically for use on mobile devices.

- *WMLScript,* a language similar to Java Script that optimises WML.

- Telephony services and programming interfaces.

- Support for images, calendars, diaries.

2.7.2 *Wireless Session Protocol* (WSP) - **Wireless session protocol**

It allows the application of an interface for establishing sessions. To this end, two different types of protocol have been created: the first for connection via the transaction service (WTP), and the other allows direct access to the WDP layer, without the need to establish a direct connection with the other layers, which improves the performance of applications that do not require confirmation of data being sent. Allows efficient data exchange between applications.

2.7.3   *Wireless* Transaction Protocol (WTP) - Wireless Transaction Protocol

It's a simplified protocol, idealised for low-bandwidth situations, which is the specific case of wireless communications.

This protocol offers three types of transaction:

- One for sending messages unchallenged by the server;

- Sending messages with notification of received messages;

- The latter is a transaction that allows messages to be sent from user to user, activating confirmation that everyone has received your message.

This protocol also allows the concatenation of messages and the induced delay of new notifications to minimise the number of messages sent.

2.7.4   *Wireless Transport Layer Security* (WTLS) - Wireless transport and security layer

Security protocol based on the industry standard TLS (**Transport Layer Security**) protocol. It provides a secure means of transport between the WAP device and the WAP **Gateway**. WTLS makes it possible to ensure that the content sent has not been manipulated by third parties. It also guarantees privacy and ensures that the author of the message will be identified.

2.7.5   *Wireless Datagram Protocol* (WDP) - Wireless Datagram Protocol

It is the layer that carries the data, responsible for sending and receiving messages over the various types of network, including SMS, GPRS and GSM. As the WDP protocol provides an interface between the higher protocols, WAE, WSP and WTLS, it is able to function independently of the telephone network it is working with, or adapt to the specifications of said network.

2.8   How the WAP security model works

For security mechanisms, the WAP protocol uses a sub-protocol called WTLS (**Wireless Transport Layer Security**). To understand how this protocol works, below is a description of how the SSL (**Security Socket Layer**) security layer works, which is responsible for economic transactions on the Internet.

The SSL protocol provides a secure environment for economic transactions on the Internet.

There are four distinct points to mention when it comes to security: privacy, integrity, authenticity and confirmation of attendance.

Privacy guarantees that only the sender and recipient of a message can access its content. To enable this, the data is encrypted. This ensures that no-one can see, access or use the information involved (e.g. addresses, credit card numbers, telephone numbers) while it is being transmitted over the Internet.

Integrity ensures that any change in the content of a message is detected from the moment it leaves the sender until it reaches the recipient. For example, if a customer orders the transfer of R$20,000.00 from his bank account to another account, integrity allows the bank and/or the customer to realise if the order has been modified along the way. There are tools that ensure that data is transmitted without any variation.

Authentication guarantees that the parties involved in a transaction are really who they say they are. Server verification serves the client to ensure that they are buying from the web server they believe they are connected to. This action assures the web server that the client is not using a false identity. One of the clearest examples of authenticity in the real world is the presentation of an identity card when asked to identify a person.

Confirmation of presence provides a method so that none of the parties involved can falsely claim that they were not present at the transaction. A clearer example of this procedure in the real world is the notarisation of a signature on a document.

This protocol will provide greater security in communications between terminals, for example in credit card authentication.

The functions of this protocol can be enabled or disabled by other applications, depending on the security needs and characteristics of the network (for example, it could be disabled in networks that already have security protocols in place).

On the Internet, the SSL Protocol digitally certifies any user and provides the four points for completing a transaction.

2.8.1　Security and the WAP environment

"As you can see in figure 9, there are two different **parts** to the WAP security model. In the partedireitadodiagramme, the WAP **Gateway** simply uses SSL to establish secure communication with the Web server, ensuring the **server's** privacy, **integrity and authentication." [Demétrio, 2000, p. 13]**

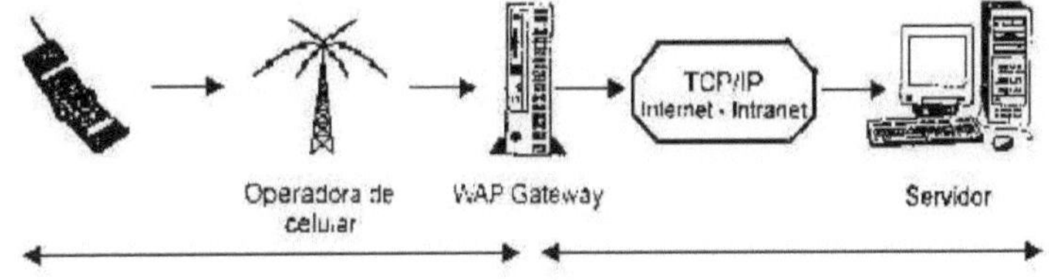

Figure 9: WAP Security Model

On the left, the **Gateway** takes the SSL-encrypted data from the web server and transforms it so that it can be transmitted, using WAP and the WTLS security protocol. Requests from the phone to the web server go the other way round. In short, the **Gateway** acts as a gateway between the WTLS and SSL protocols.

The need to convert between SSL and WTLS is imposed by the nature of wireless communications: reduced bandwidth, since the SSL protocol was created to be used by personal computers with more processing power than a mobile phone and greater bandwidth. Manufacturers could include the SSL protocol in mobile phones, but this could drive up the price of handsets, slowing down the growth of the WAP industry.

The WTLS protocol has been specifically designed for a sufficient level of security without requiring a great deal of processing power.

The transformation between SSL and WTLS takes only a few milliseconds and takes place in the **Gateway**'s memory simultaneously with hundreds or thousands of other requests, allowing for a secure connection between all protocols.

WAP **Gateway** developers and network operators take all possible measures to keep the WAP **Gateway** secure:

- *Gateway* never stores the decoded content on some kind of secondary medium.

- The encoding/decoding process has been developed according to optimised security parameters with such speed that the original content will be erased from the *Gateway*'s volatile memory as soon as possible.

2.9 How SSL works

The key element of the SSL protocol is a public encryption code. This uses a pair of codes and mathematical algorithms that convert plain text into encrypted text and vice versa. This pair of codes consists of a public registered code and a private one, which is kept secret by the owner. A message encoded with the public code can only be decoded with the private code. The reverse is true. Just like a door that can only be

31

opened with two keys.

Public code encryption is very useful for small amounts of data, but becomes slow when large amounts are used. For the latter case, private or symmetric encryption is used.

"The SSL protocol combines both techniques to carry out transactions. In a first contact, known as a negotiation, the sender and recipient will communicate using the public code, which will ensure privacy during the rest of the transaction.

To ensure integrity, the SSL protocol uses algorithms that create a mathematical digital signature for each message. If the message changes along the way, the recipient will see that the digital signature does not match the message and will reject it.

The authenticity of both parties is confirmed through digital certificates, which prevent a third party from intercepting the transmissions. The certificates ensure that the sender and recipient are who they say they are.

When the browser requests a connection with a server, the server displays its certificate. The browser checks to see if the certificate is valid; if so, it proceeds with the transaction and then encodes/decodes the data." [Demétrio, 2000, p.13]

2.10   Wap Languages - Wml and Wmlscript

2.10.1   The WML Language

The WAP specification defines WML (**Wireless Markup Language**), a language based on XML, which is used to create pages for devices that use WAP technology, such as mobile phones and palmtops.

2.10.2   WML includes four main functional areas

Text presentation and layout: WML includes text and image support, including a variety of formatting commands. You can create bold text, for example.

Organisation in cards and decks: all the information in WML is organised in a collection of cards and **decks**. Cards specify one or more units of user interaction (for example, a selection menu, a text screen or a text input field). Logically, a user navigates through a series of WML cards, examining the contents by entering data, making choices and moving between cards.

Grouping: Cards are grouped together within **decks**. A **deck** is similar to an HTML page, which is identified by a URL.

Navigation and links between cards: includes navigation management between cards and **decks**. It also supports anchored **links** on the page, similar to HTML.

2.11   The WMLScript language

"WMLScript *(Wireless Markup Language Script)* is a *scripting* language that is executed on the client. It makes up for the shortcomings of WML, as is the case with *JavaScript* and HTML. It makes WML pages more robust. Like WML, *WMLScript* has undergone some modifications to adapt to the limitations of the WAP environment, and is very limited compared to *JavaScript.* " **[Demétrio, 2000, p.16]**

2.12   The Microbrowser

This is the programme responsible for interpreting the WML and *WMLScript* languages and displaying them on the screen. It is stored on the WAP mobile phone. It does not allow access to HTML content, the language in which web pages are created. Some *microbrowsers* incorporate the functions of searching and storing favourites in their own folder.

2.13   The Sites

The mobile phone views the site via a *microbrowser*, which is a reduced version of the browsers used for the web. The *microbrowser* is used to visualise the site's content (usually text, some images and a menu layout) and to use services (such as forms). Each *microbrowser* has its own characteristics, so the same page can be viewed differently in different *microbrowsers,* in the same way that web browsers view pages with slight differences. With the *microbrowser*, you can use all the services that you are used to on the web and are part of everyday life, such as online shops, portals, diaries, email, as long as they have been built for WAP technology.

"**All companies that want to make** their services, products and information **available** via mobile phones will have to create WAP **micro-sites**. This will generate a flourishing new labour market for **webmasters,** programmers, consultants, journalists and **information technology** professionals." **[www.palmland.com.br]**

Sites that have not been built in WML can also be accessed, but only sites specific to WAP technology can guarantee that you will be able to view them and use the services.

One of the layers of the WAP protocol, WTLS, provides encryption and authentication for secure transactions between client and server. This feature prevents unauthorised access to WAP transactions, paving the way for e-commerce via mobile phones.

CHAPTER 3

Wireless Technologies

This chapter will show you some **wireless** technologies that, in one way or another, influence the WAP process.

3.1 Bluetooth **Technology**

3.1.1 Concept

According to Demétrio (2000, p.22), "with this technology it is possible to quickly and easily **connect** an extensive range of devices, without the need for cables, making use of a low range connection. This extends the capability of laptops, mobile phones and other mobile devices, both inside and outside the office. Using a low-frequency radio transmission, this cable-free connection can be established. The elimination of cables, which are currently widely used to transfer information, is one of the main reasons for adopting this technology."

The biggest telecoms and IT companies, the SIG (**Bluetooth** Special Interest Group), formed in 1998 by Ericsson, IBM, Intel, Nokia and Toshiba, control the development of **Bluetooth** technology, which is innovative and was developed with the growing need for truly cheap, economical and global wireless communications in mind.

SIG is the result of the global commitment of the five founding companies that manage the development of the technology and its subsequent incorporation into the market.

3.1.2 Operation

Basically, it works as follows: you equip a device with a microchip which, in turn, will make it act in a similar way to a low-range **walkie-talkie**.

Using short-range radio signals emitted by the microchip, the device scans its surroundings for other devices that are also equipped with **Bluetooth** technology.

Once positive recognition has been established, an exchange of information between these devices begins.

3.1.3 **Typical usage situations**

"How about a three-in-one phone and an application to automatically synchronise a PDA, a phone and a micro laptop. The three-in-one works like a normal cordless phone when it's within range of the base. When it leaves the range of the base, it behaves like a mobile phone. Another function is when the phone is in range of another three-in-one phone. Both phones can act as if they were walkie-talkies, but they don't need to be connected to the telephone network. [Demétrio, 2000, p.23]

They could also be connected to a mobile phone, palm or notebook. A contact list, personal and professional diary could be constantly updated automatically.

In lectures and meetings, it would be possible to send the content of your presentation directly from your PC to the projector, without going through that tangle of wires.

3.2   GSM (Global System for Mobile Communications)

"The future has arrived and brought with it many of the things that until then had only been a reality in science fiction films." [Demétrio, 2000, p.23]

That said, we can talk about the GSM communication system, the technology on which the WAP protocol is based. This communication system is based on radio transmissions that allow digital access to the telephone network from mobile devices.

One of the great features of GSM is its capacity for digital communication between the device and the receiving station, which allows the transmitted data to be encrypted, making communication more secure and of better quality. It even allows a packet of lost data to be sent back to the sender to retrieve the information not received.

3.2.1   GSM operation

"Because it's a digital network, it means that radio waves propagate through the air, just as webs travel through a spider's web, with all due respect. What's more, GSM is a cellular network, which means it's divided into small cells. A cell is nothing more than a coverage area that a receiving station covers. In this way, you can have stations and terminals that aren't very powerful (covering an area of a few kilometres), with the possibility of adding more cells to your network, depending on the need to expand coverage to new geographical regions.

These cells are connected to each other (usually by cable, sometimes by radio waves) and all of them are connected to the *Gateway* that communicates with the fixed telephony network." [Demétrio, 2000, p.23 and 24]

As it is a cellular network, it is always possible to increase the number of cells and decrease their size to increase the capacity of the network as a whole.

One of the advantages of GSM is the ability to identify the user on the network. In this way, you don't have to rely on a single terminal, and you can use any other terminal to carry out communications.

When you connect to the Internet from your mobile phone, the network does a short check to verify the user, then searches the available GSM networks and validates the communication on one of them (usually the contracted one). From there, the nearest cell will provide coverage and be able to send and receive information.

"So far so good, but what if you're in another state or country, too far away from your operator, can you still surf the Internet with your mobile phone? It's possible, using a technique called *roaming,* which allows you to use the network of another operator with which you have a prior agreement. This way you can travel with your WAP mobile phone without worrying about coverage.

It's worth mentioning a second case that can occur when browsing on a mobile phone. Imagine browsing a WAP site while driving to the coast in a car at 80 kilometres per hour.

During your journey, you may cross an area covered by several cells in full navigation mode. Of course, navigation should not be interrupted and the change from one cell to another should not be noticeable to the user. The process responsible for this transaction is called hand-over, which allows you to change cells and even GSM networks without losing communication." [Demétrio, 2000, p.24]

The GSM standard has more than 200 million users in more than 100 countries and offers good quality Internet access. Everything indicates that it will be the standard adopted in Brazil.

3.3   GPRS

GPRS (**General Packet Radio Service**) is a service that allows you to send and receive information using a mobile phone network.

It has nothing to do with GPS (**Global Position System**), a technology also used in mobile devices.

It makes it possible to reach speeds three times faster than the current fixed-line network and ten times faster than GSM. It facilitates instant connections as quickly as you need to send and receive information. You can say that using GPRS you are always connected.

Due to the higher speed, current applications could perform better and catapult new applications.

To access this service, you need a phone that supports GPRS (the current ones don't yet), and an operator that has a GPRS network, as long as you allow free access to the network.

3.3.1   GPRS operation

It works relatively simply. The information sent or received is broken down into packets and reassembled when it reaches its destination.

"To give you a clear idea of how it works, imagine this: you go to a shop and buy a wardrobe that you've seen on display. When it's delivered, the wardrobe is dismantled and then assembled in the house.

This operation, together with others specific to this network, allows it to achieve high data transmission speeds." [Demétrio, 2000, p.25]

Another example of a network that sends information in packets is the Internet.

GPRS allows full connection to all current Internet services, which will enable current operators to become content providers.

3.4 SMS

SMS *(Short Message Service)* - Short Message Service is the ability to send and receive text messages on mobile phones.

You can send alphanumeric characters or numbers and even a combination of the two.

"SMS was developed in the first part of the GSM standard. It is believed that the first short message was sent from a computer to a mobile phone in England in December 1992." [Demétrio, 2000, p.26]

3.4.1 Message characteristics

A short message text can be up to 160 characters long when the alphabet is of Latin origin, but only 70 when it is not of Latin origin, for example the Arabic and Chinese alphabets.

Currently, this service is used not only for communications between users, but also to send a large amount of information to users, such as information on fares, flights, various news items and the weather forecast.

It's safe to say that SMS is already a hit with users in Europe, with millions of messages exchanged in 1999.

It is also possible to send and receive e-mail through this system, where the telephone number itself becomes part of the customer's e-mail address.

An e-mail is sent to the user using the short message service. It will be very useful in places where the Internet has little or no penetration.

This technology is another revolution that is being very well accepted in the places where it has been implemented.

Here in Brazil, some operators have recently made the service available only to mobile phones that have the technology, but they promise to repeat Europe's success. It should soon become a fever among teenagers, business people and anyone who needs to exchange information quickly.

3.5 MMS (Multimedia Message Service)

MMS refers to the service that allows you to send and receive messages with multimedia content, and is seen by operators and other players in the sector as the natural evolution of mobile messaging. From the point of view of mobile customers, this evolution provides a significant improvement in the experience of using services from their mobile terminal, and therefore represents a business opportunity for developers of solutions that take advantage of this technology. MMS combines the three success factors of the modern era of media consumption: speed of access, personalisation, audio and image capabilities.

Skills required:

- Knowledge of HTTP (Hypertext Transfer Protocol) and PAP (Push Access Protocol)

- SMIL language, in case the external application wants to process complex multimedia messages, i.e. containing more than a single image.

In short, the localisation component opens up a window of opportunity for mobile operators to differentiate themselves from the competition, an area in which partners who develop applications and services can play a leading role.

Skills required:

Knowledge of HTTP (Hypertext Transfer Protocol) and XML (eXtended Markup Language)

Running Java applications on mobile terminals is one of the latest and most important technological capabilities on the market, as it substantially improves the user experience when using and viewing services.

"Optimus has a Provisioning Platform, where various types of content are hosted, such as the Java Games on offer from Optimus, for customers to download to their terminals. Given the flexibility of the platform, other types of partner content can be hosted on the same platform, such as Java (J2ME - Java 2 Micro Edition), Symbian and Smartphone applications." [www.optimus.pt]

In Brazil, MMS is already a reality. During the finals of the Brazilian Championship, for example, the operator TIM, in partnership with Folha Online, sent a group of subscribers photos of the goals scored by

Santos and Corinthians during the game. It was the first test of an MMS news service in Latin America

It's clear that it will have to overcome the natural maturing process of a telecommunications service, but in the medium term it should evolve in a similar way to the SMS text messaging service, which is now popular with mobile phone users in Brazil and around the world.

"Even so, experts point to MMS as a "cash cow" for operators of 2.5G networks, which use the GPRS (Global Packet Radio Service) system - the technology for sending data packets at high speeds. GPRS is the natural evolution of the GSM system.

Despite the good speed, research shows that sending photos, exchanging messages and downloading screensavers are the MMS applications with the greatest potential for success in the market. More complex applications, such as downloading videos and interactive games, are not perceived as the main revenue generators, at least at first. But operators are already considering offering these services in Brazil too." [www1.folha.uol.com.br]

CHAPTER 4

Current panorama of cellular systems in Brazil

Table 3: Mobile Cellular Service Providers

Operators	Operator websites	Technology*	Band	Type of Grant
Claro (Telecom Américas)	América Móvil, Americel, Claro digital, Claro, ATL, Tess	TDMA and GSM	B,D,E	SMP
TIM	TIM BRAZIL, TIM NORTHEAST, TIM SOUTH	TDMA and GSM	A,B,D,E	SMP
Live	LIVE	TDMA and CDMA	A,B	SMP
Amazon and Telemig Celular	Amazônia Celular, Telemig Celular	TDMA	A	SMC
BCP	BCP	TDMA	B	SMC
CTBC Celular	CTBC CELULAR	TDMA	A	SMC
Sercomtel Mobile phone	Sercomtel Celular	TDMA	A	SMP
Oi (Telemar)	OI	GSM	D	SMP
Brasil Telecom	Brasil Telecom	GSM	E	SMP
Vesper	Vesper	CDMA	E	SMP

* Data technology: GPRS (GSM operators) 1xRTT (Vivo).

CHAPTER 5

Conclusions

Mobile communications are currently revolutionising telecoms services and the way people use them. The demand for wireless telephony and data services with satisfactory coverage has grown beyond expectations, and forecasts are that demand will continue to grow.

This is reflected in engineering activities, which are committed to designing new systems with more advantageous features for the user, developing ways of integrating existing services and mechanisms and techniques to increase efficiency in the use of resources. This development is necessary to meet new demands not only from users, but also from new applications.

With this, it can be seen that mobile communications represent a discontinuity in telecommunications services and technologies, whose future development will involve a game between market forces, regulatory bodies, technological innovations and existing standards and those under study. The road to achieving a complete vision of communication services will be revolutionary, and the rate and direction of this evolution will depend on the battle mentioned above.

The need to bring the facilities offered by the Internet domain to the mobile environment in order to add value to products initially led companies in the sector to race to come up with the best solution. However, it was soon realised that isolated attempts would lead to conflicts and fragmentation of the market, so they joined forces in a forum with the aim of producing a single alternative to the problem.

In order to increase productivity and the assimilation of concepts, we chose to follow a model that has already been widely discussed and disseminated: the Internet model.

The WAP standard was produced on the basis of the protocols of the TCP/IP stack, enhanced in such a way as to meet/address the restrictions that exist in the operating environment of wireless networks.

Bibliographical references

DEMÉTRIO, Rinaldo. *W@P Technology - Learn how to create pages for mobile phones using the WML language.* São Paulo: Editora Érica, 2000, 1" edition.

VIEIRA, M. Carlos Alexandre. *Wired Internet*. Osasco: UNIFIEO, 2000. (Monograph)

CABRAL, Jorge Luiz. *Security in WAP Transactions and Applications. Campanha Region*: URCAMP, 2000. (Monograph)

Electronic Publications

http://www.wapforum.org (03/10/2017)

http://www.wapmine.com (11/10/2017)

http://www.waptastic.com (11/10/2017)

http://www.folhawap.com.br (08/10/2016)

http://www. vivo.com. br (10/02/2018)

http://www.uolwap.uol.com.br/metrics1.php (03/03/2018)

http://www.3g.com.br (03/03/2018)

http://www.palmland.com.br (10/04/2018)

http://www.testecell.hpg.ig.com.br/wap.htm(10/04/2018)

http://www.palmland.com.br/wap/wap.asp (05/05/2018)

http://www.optimus.pt (05/07/2018)

http://www1.folha.uol.com.br (12/07/2016)

GLOSSARY

Mobile Phone Coverage Area: Territorial extension reached by the signals of a Base Radio Station.

Mobile Phone Mobility Area: This is the **area** in which you can move around freely, paying a single local mobile phone communication fee, without incurring additional costs per call or journey.

Mobile Phone Registration Area: Region in which a mobile phone has been registered.

Shadow Area: Places within a service area where obstacles - such as walls, buildings, viaducts, mountains or dense vegetation - block the propagation of radio waves, preventing communication between base stations and mobile handsets.

Band (A or B): Radio frequency band concession for the operation of the Mobile Cellular Service, assigned to a state-owned or private telephone company.

Mailbox: The place where messages recorded by the Mobile Voice Mail are stored.

Cell: Geographical area covered by a Base Radio Station (BRS).

Portable mobile phone: The most widely used device, as it is the most practical because it fits in the palm of your hand and allows for greater mobility.

Transportable mobile phone: Larger and heavier than a portable mobile phone, with greater power resulting in better range and longer battery operating time. **In-car mobile phone:** A device installed in the car's console, whose power source is always the car's battery. They have five times more power than portable mobile phones.

Switching and Control Centre (CCC): Equipment responsible for controlling the reception and transmission of calls made by mobile phones.

Voicemail: Service that works like an answering machine in the Mobile Cellular Service.

Display: Display of the mobile phone handset that shows all the information related to the operation of the handset and also shows all the commands made.

Mobile Station (MS): Equipment (vehicular, transportable or portable) that allows its user to interconnect with the public telephone network or with another mobile station.

Base Radio Station (BTS): Towers containing equipment for receiving and transmitting signals (radio waves) emitted by mobile phones.

Habilitation: Includes the procedures relating to the programming of the telephone number assigned to the customer, in order to activate their mobile phone and start providing the mobile service.

Home: On the Mobile handset, this means that you are in the area where your mobile phone has been registered.

Microcells: These are micro-antennas that amplify the cellular signal reception condition designed to serve places with a high traffic density, such as airports, **shopping malls**, convention centres and intersections of large avenues.

No Service: Information that appears on the mobile phone display whenever the user is in a location with a weak signal level (garages, mountains).

Protocol: a set of rules governing the format and meaning of frames, packets or messages exchanged between partner organisations within the same layer. Protocols are used to implement services and are not directly visible to users, i.e. the protocol used can be modified as long as the service offered to the user remains the same.

Accredited Network: Retail shops or mobile handset dealers throughout the state of São Paulo, authorised to sell, qualify and exchange mobile handsets, including in cases of theft, robbery or loss.

Signal Repeaters: Small antennas that guarantee a signal for mobile phone calls and offer better quality in areas where signal propagation is difficult. They are installed in tunnels, restaurants and hotels.

Roam: Information that appears on the mobile phone display whenever the user is outside the registration area.

Roaming: System that allows the user to make or receive calls outside the area where the mobile phone was registered.

Automatic Roaming: Automatic registration of a subscriber who is outside their area of registration with the Switching and Control Centre (CCC) of the area being visited.

Supplementary Services: Additional **services** that make your communications even more dynamic.

Analogue Mobile Cellular System: This is the system in which the user's voice is transformed by the mobile handset into continuous electrical signals and transmitted over radio waves.

Digital Mobile Cellular System: This is the system in which the user's voice is transformed by the mobile handset into bits (zeros and ones - binary code used by computers) and transmitted in this way via radio waves.

Digital Cellular Mobile System - CDMA: (Code Division Multiple Access) - This is the system in which several conversations are transmitted simultaneously on the same radio frequency channel and in the same time interval; however, each conversation receives an identification code that differentiates it from the others.

Digital Mobile Cellular System - TDMA: (Time Division Multiple Access) - This is the system in which several conversations are transmitted simultaneously on the same radio frequency channel; however, each conversation is transmitted at different time intervals. In this system, conversations are not coded, as the radio frequency channels are differentiated by time interval.

Printed by Books on Demand GmbH, Norderstedt / Germany